Francis Frith's
AROUND HARROGATE

PHOTOGRAPHIC MEMORIES

Francis Frith's
AROUND HARROGATE

Clive Hardy

First published in the United Kingdom in 2000 by
Frith Book Company Ltd

Hardback Edition 2000
ISBN 1-85937-112-4

Paperback Edition 2001
ISBN 1-85937-423-9

Reprinted in Hardback 2001

British Library Cataloguing in Publication Data

Francis Frith's Around Harrogate
Clive Hardy

Frith Book Company Ltd
Frith's Barn, Teffont,
Salisbury, Wiltshire SP3 5QP
Tel: +44 (0) 1722 716 376
Email: info@frithbook.co.uk
www.frithbook.co.uk

Printed and bound in Great Britain

As with any historical database the Frith archive is constantly being corrected and improved and the publishers would welcome information on omissions or inaccuracies

Contents

FRANCIS FRITH: *Victorian Pioneer*

FRANCIS FRITH, Victorian founder of the world-famous photographic archive, was a complex and multitudinous man. A devout Quaker and a highly successful Victorian businessman, he was both philosophic by nature and pioneering in outlook.

By 1855 Francis Frith had already established a wholesale grocery business in Liverpool, and sold it for the astonishing sum of £200,000, which is the equivalent today of over £15,000,000. Now a multi-millionaire, he was able to indulge his passion for travel. As a child he had pored over travel books written by early explorers, and his fancy and imagination had been stirred by family holidays to the sublime mountain regions of Wales and Scotland. 'What a land of spirit-stirring and enriching scenes and places!' he had written. He was to return to these scenes of grandeur in later years to 'recapture the thousands of vivid and tender memories', but with a different purpose. Now in his thirties, and captivated by the new science of photography, Frith set out on a series of pioneering journeys to the Nile regions that occupied him from 1856 until 1860.

INTRIGUE AND ADVENTURE

He took with him on his travels a specially-designed wicker carriage that acted as both dark-room and sleeping chamber. These far-flung journeys were packed with intrigue and adventure. In his life story, written when he was sixty-three, Frith tells of being held captive by bandits, and of fighting 'an awful midnight battle to the very point of surrender with a deadly pack of hungry, wild dogs'. Sporting flowing Arab costume, Frith arrived at Akaba by camel seventy years before Lawrence, where he encountered 'desert princes and rival sheikhs, blazing with jewel-hilted swords'.

During these extraordinary adventures he was assiduously exploring the desert regions bordering the Nile and patiently recording the antiquities and peoples with his camera. He was the first photographer to venture beyond the sixth cataract. Africa was still the mysterious 'Dark Continent', and Stanley and Livingstone's historic meeting was a decade into the future. The conditions for picture taking confound belief. He laboured for hours in his wicker dark-room in the sweltering heat of the desert, while the volatile chemicals fizzed dangerously in their trays. Often he was forced to work in remote tombs and caves where conditions were cooler. Back in London he exhibited his photographs and was 'rapturously cheered' by members of the Royal Society. His reputation as a photographer was made overnight. An eminent modern historian has likened their impact on the population of the time to that on our own generation of the first photographs taken on the surface of the moon.

Venture of a Life-Time

Characteristically, Frith quickly spotted the opportunity to create a new business as a specialist publisher of photographs. He lived in an era of immense and sometimes violent change. For the poor in the early part of Victoria's reign work was a drudge and the hours long, and people had precious little free time to enjoy themselves.

Most had no transport other than a cart or gig at their disposal, and had not travelled far beyond the boundaries of their own town or village. However, by the 1870s, the railways had threaded their way across the country, and Bank Holidays and half-day Saturdays had been made obligatory by Act of Parliament. All of a sudden the ordinary working man and his family were able to enjoy days out and see a little more of the world.

With characteristic business acumen, Francis Frith foresaw that these new tourists would enjoy having souvenirs to commemorate their days out. In 1860 he married Mary Ann Rosling and set out with the intention of photographing every city, town and village in Britain. For the next thirty years he travelled the country by train and by pony and trap, producing fine photographs of seaside resorts and beauty spots that were keenly bought by millions of Victorians. These prints were painstakingly pasted into family albums and pored over during the dark nights of winter, rekindling precious memories of summer excursions.

The Rise of Frith & Co

Frith's studio was soon supplying retail shops all over the country. To meet the demand he gathered about him a small team of photographers, and published the work of independent artist-photographers of the calibre of Roger Fenton and Francis Bedford. In order to gain some understanding of the scale of Frith's business one only has to look at the catalogue issued by Frith & Co in 1886: it runs to some 670

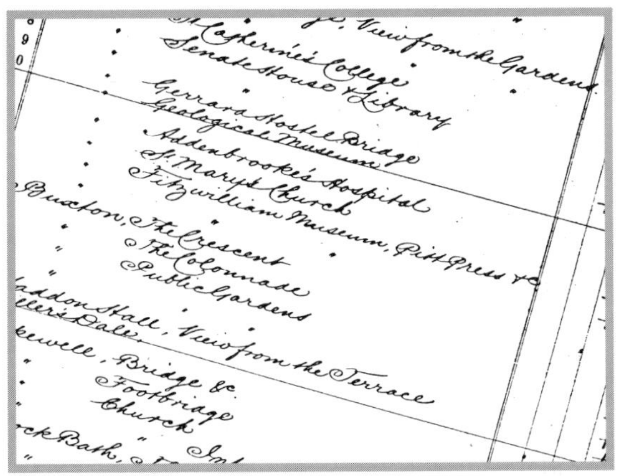
View from the Garden
Catherine's College
Senate House & Library
Gerrard Hostel Bridge
Geological Museum
Addenbrooke's Hospital
St Mary's Church
Fitzwilliam Museum, Pitt Press &
Buxton, The Crescent
The Colonnade
Public Gardens
Haddon Hall, View from the Terrace
Bridge &c.
Footbridge
Church

pages, listing not only many thousands of views of the British Isles but also many photographs of most European countries, and China, Japan, the USA and Canada – note the sample page shown above from the hand-written *Frith & Co* ledgers detailing pictures taken. By 1890 Frith had created the greatest specialist photographic publishing company in the world, with over 2,000 outlets – more than the combined number that Boots and WH Smith have today! The picture on the right shows the *Frith & Co* display board at Ingleton in the Yorkshire Dales. Beautifully constructed with mahogany frame and gilt inserts, it could display up to a dozen local scenes.

Postcard Bonanza

The ever-popular holiday postcard we know today took many years to develop. In 1870 the Post Office issued the first plain cards, with a pre-printed stamp on one face. In 1894 they allowed other publishers' cards to be sent through the mail with an attached adhesive halfpenny stamp. Demand grew rapidly, and in 1895 a new size of postcard was permitted called the court card, but there was little room for illustration. In 1899, a year after Frith's death, a new card measuring 5.5 x 3.5 inches became the standard format, but it was not until 1902 that the divided back came into being, with address and message on one face and a full-size illustration on the other. *Frith & Co* were in the vanguard of postcard development, and Frith's sons Eustace and Cyril continued their father's monumental task, expanding the number of views offered to the public and recording more and more places in Britain, as the coasts and countryside were opened up to mass travel.

Francis Frith died in 1898 at his villa in Cannes, his great project still growing. The archive he created continued in business for another seventy years. By 1970 it contained over a third of a million pictures of 7,000 cities, towns and villages. The massive photographic record Frith has left to us stands as a living monument to a special and very remarkable man.

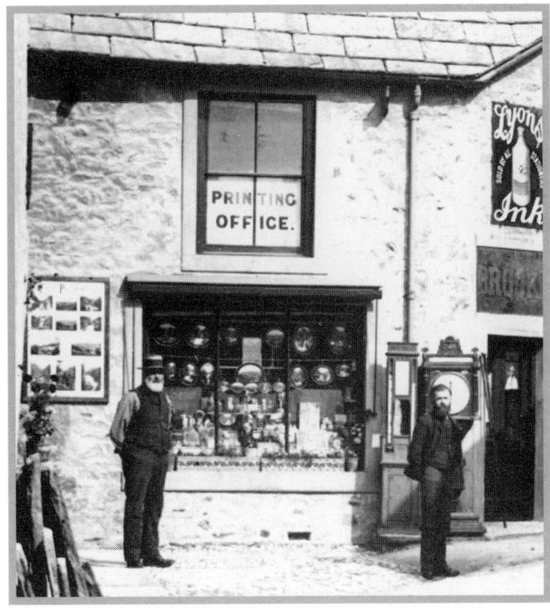

Frith's Archive: *A Unique Legacy*

Francis Frith's legacy to us today is of immense significance and value, for the magnificent archive of evocative photographs he created provides a unique record of change in 7,000 cities, towns and villages throughout Britain over a century and more. Frith and his fellow studio photographers revisited locations many times down the years to update their views, compiling for us an enthralling and colourful pageant of British life and character.

We tend to think of Frith's sepia views of Britain as nostalgic, for most of us use them to conjure up memories of places in our own lives with which we have family associations. It often makes us forget that to Francis Frith they were records of daily life as it was actually being lived in the cities, towns and villages of his day. The Victorian age was one of great and often bewildering change for ordinary people, and though the pictures evoke an impression of slower times, life was as busy and hectic as it is today.

We are fortunate that Frith was a photographer of the people, dedicated to recording the minutiae of everyday life. For it is this sheer wealth of visual data, the painstaking chronicle of changes in dress, transport, street layouts, buildings, housing, engineering and landscape that captivates us so much today. His remarkable images offer us a powerful link with the past and with the lives of our ancestors.

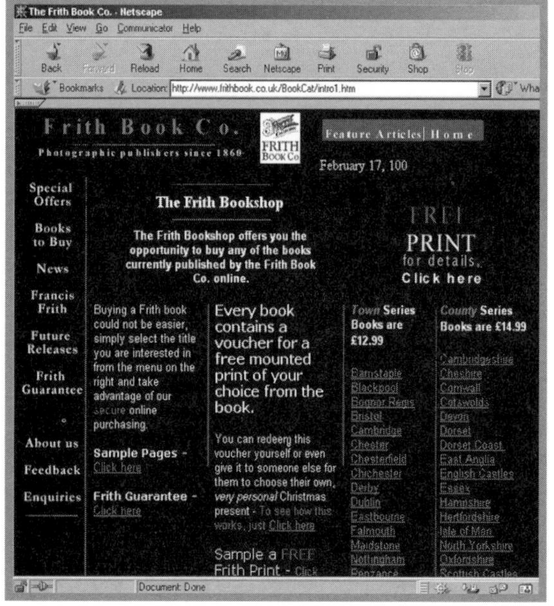

See Frith at www. frithbook.co.uk

Today's Technology

Computers have now made it possible for Frith's many thousands of images to be accessed almost instantly. In the Frith archive today, each photograph is carefully 'digitised' then stored on a CD Rom. Frith archivists can locate a single photograph amongst thousands within seconds. Views can be catalogued and sorted under a variety of categories of place and content to the immediate benefit of researchers. Inexpensive reference prints can be created for them at the touch of a mouse button, and a wide range of books and other printed materials assembled and published for a wider, more general readership - in the next twelve months over a hundred Frith local history titles will be published! The day-to-day workings of the archive are very different from how they were in Francis Frith's time: imagine the herculean task of sorting through eleven tons of glass negatives as Frith had to do to locate a particular sequence of pictures! Yet the archive still prides itself on maintaining the same high standards of excellence laid down by Francis Frith, including the painstaking cataloguing and indexing of every view.

It is curious to reflect on how the internet now allows researchers in America and elsewhere greater instant access to the archive than Frith himself ever enjoyed. Many thousands of individual views can be called up on screen within seconds on one of the Frith internet sites, enabling people living continents away to revisit the streets of their ancestral home town, or view places in Britain where they have enjoyed holidays. Many overseas researchers welcome the chance to view special theme selections, such as transport, sports, costume and ancient monuments.

We are certain that Francis Frith would have heartily approved of these modern developments, for he himself was always working at the very limits of Victorian photographic technology.

The Value of the Archive Today

Because of the benefits brought by the computer, Frith's images are increasingly studied by social historians, by researchers into genealogy and ancestory, by architects, town planners, and by teachers and schoolchildren involved in local history projects. In addition, the archive offers every one of us a unique opportunity to examine the places where we and our families have lived and worked down the years. Immensely successful in Frith's own era, the archive is now, a century and more on, entering a new phase of popularity.

The Past in Tune with the Future

Historians consider the Francis Frith Collection to be of prime national importance. It is the only archive of its kind remaining in private ownership and has been valued at a million pounds. However, this figure is now rapidly increasing as digital technology enables more and more people around the world to enjoy its benefits.

Francis Frith's archive is now housed in an historic timber barn in the beautiful village of Teffont in Wiltshire. Its founder would not recognize the archive office as it is today. In place of the many thousands of dusty boxes containing glass plate negatives and an all-pervading odour of photographic chemicals, there are now ranks of computer screens. He would be amazed to watch his images travelling round the world at unimaginable speeds through network and internet lines.

The archive's future is both bright and exciting. Francis Frith, with his unshakeable belief in making photographs available to the greatest number of people, would undoubtedly approve of what is being done today with his lifetime's work. His photographs, depicting our shared past, are now bringing pleasure and enlightenment to millions around the world a century and more after his death.

Around Harrogate – *An Introduction*

Harrogate is one of the oldest and most favourite of the English spa towns. The curative mineral springs were discovered by Sir William Slingsby in 1571. Slingsby's discovery was different, in that it was the first spring not connected with the holy wells of old. In Slingsby's day the town of Harrogate did not exist: the area was moorland within the Royal Forest of Knaresborough, and Harrogate was within the township of Bilton. By the middle of the 17th century the sulphur well was in use, and when naturalist John Ray visited it in 1661 he wrote that 'though it be pellucid enough, yet it stinks noisomely, like rotten eggs'.

The 200-acre Stray was opened for public use in 1778, but a number of local families retained grazing rights, or gates, as they were called. There were fifty gates, each entitling the owner to graze either one cow, or a two-year-old horse, or four sheep. Gates were property, and as such could be bought and sold or rented out. William Sheepshanks, who became one of Harrogate's leading landowners, acquired a number of gates and was wealthy enough to pay for the building of Christ Church. All animals on the Stray were looked after by a herdsman. In Christ Church there is the tombstone of William Hill, who was the Stray herdsman for forty years. William's job would have been to attend to all animals legitimately placed on the Stray by the gate holders. His duty was to exclude donkeys, mules, pigs, goats and geese, and he was empowered to impound any animal grazing illegally - or gate-crashing, as it was known.

A hospital for diseases considered treatable with spa waters had opened on Cornwall Road in 1826, and by the mid 19th century the Bath Hospital had 40 beds. Unfortunately, during the summer months there was often a conflict of interest: visitors appear to have received preferential treatment over locals. This was eventually solved by closing the hospital down until the season had finished. In the 1880s it was decided to replace the Bath with a new all-year-round 150-bed hospital. Designed by T Worthington & Elgood of Manchester, the Royal Bath Hospital and Rawson Convalescent Home was completed in 1889. The total cost was in the region of £50,000; the £13,000 Convalescent Home was paid for by Miss Elizabeth Rawson and the Hon H E Butler of Nidd Hall.

By the early decades of the 19th century Harrogate was a fashionable place. Though its full potential would not be realised until the Duchy of Lancaster took an active role in developing facilities in the 1840s, by the 1850s Harrogate was considered to be the smartest inland spa in England. In 1821 Edward Baines had written: 'to this place during the summer months the nobility and gentry resort from all parts of Great Britain and Ireland, to receive the benefit of the waters, for which it is so deservedly celebrated. The situation of the place with respect of the circumjacent country, is high and commanding, and the air is of course cool and salubrious. High Harrogate commands a most excellent prospect of the surrounding country, finely varied by towns, villages, fields and plantations'.

Baines also mentioned a certain Dr Monro, who 'in treating of the sulphur waters, observes, that in small quantities they are good alternatives, and when drank in large quantities, are strongly purgative; they have been much used and found extremely serviceable in cutaneous disorders and scrofulous cases; and among the best remedies for destroying worms and their nidus, and extremely beneficial in removing indigestion and disorders arising from obstructions. Besides its internal use the sulphur water taken from the Bog Wells is much in use for warm baths, for the relief of chronic and cutaneous disorders'. During the season the Sulphur Well in Low Harrogate would be busy from 7.00am to 9.00am, surrounded by visitors eager to be served by the female attendants who dished the water out in pint glasses. The water was taken in doses of one to four pints, depending upon what needed to be cured or cleaned out. Even in 1821 people did not have to travel to Harrogate for the water: a Mr Blackburn, proprietor of the promenade rooms, already had a thriving business bottling it.

Harrogate was in fact divided into two separate parts. High Harrogate on the ridge above the Stray was in the parish of Knaresborough; Low Harrogate on the western slope of the ridge and in the valley was in the parish of Pannal. The town's name is thought to derive from the word 'Haywragate', meaning the road passing near

Hayra (modern-day Haverah). In 1821 many residents in both places made a few pounds extra during the season by taking in lodgers, but only a few offered board. Many were retailers and tradespeople, such as stonemason Benjamin Winterburn; boot and shoemaker Thomas Clark; fishmonger Thomas Hoadley; milliner Dorothy Alderson; toy and perfumery dealer Ann Pulleyn; and coach and harness maker Thomas Percy. Others, such as Elizabeth Agar, Elizabeth Kay, Christina Calvert and John Parker, appear to have had no other source of employment. There were a number of hotels offering day board and lodging, as it was then called. In High Harrogate was the Granby at 8s 6d a day full board; the Dragon, Queen's Head and Hattersley's Hotel all charged 7s 6d; and bringing up the rear was the Hope at 6s. In Lower Harrogate the most expensive hotel was the Crown at 8s 6d a day; the White Hart was 7s 6d; the Swan and the Crescent charged 6s; and the Wellington, Promenade and Binn's all charged 5s.

Three stagecoaches operated daily scheduled services. The Tally Ho and the Royal Telegraph ran from Gascoigne's, and the Union from Joseph Waite's Black Swan. Both places were in High Harrogate. The Royal Telegraph ran between Leeds and Newcastle, the other two on services to Leeds and Ripon. In the season a coach service operated to York on Mondays, Wednesdays, and Fridays. Land carriages ran between Harrogate and Leeds from the Horse & Jockey and the White Hart, and Pickersgill & Sons operated scheduled freight services to Leeds and Ripon.

In 1850 an early practitioner of a type of treatment that would later be associated with hydropathic establishments opened his consulting rooms at Volta House on Station Parade. 'Professor' W Hardy's electric baths involved giving his patients what were reputedly mild doses of electricity when they were in a bath of water or seated on a chair. By 1874 the professor's selling point was his claim to be the 'sole possessor of the Electric Steam Douche'.

The hydropathic movement well and truly arrived with the opening of the Harrogate

Hydro in 1878. Hydropathic treatments originated in Germany in the 1830s; they had the advantage of using ordinary cold water, which meant that hydros could be, and were, opened all over the place. The Harrogate was extended in 1892, the same year that another large establishment, the Cairn, opened for business. This was followed in 1893 by the town's other large hydro, the Harlow Manor, converted from architect John Milling's private residence. There were a number of smaller hydros, including the Connaught and the Imperial.

At the beginning of the 20th century the guidebooks were describing Harrogate as being 'with Bath and Buxton among the three chief inland watering-places of England. It consists of two parts, High and Low Harrogate, the former to the left (E.) of the station, the latter to the right. It is perhaps the most aristocratic of all the great English spas, and the one least exposed to the inroads of excursionists'. The sulphur springs, of which there were two strong and seventeen mild, were said to be efficacious '... for most affectations of the liver, jaundice, gout, rheumatism, and diseases of the skin. The six chalybeate springs are tonic and stimulant. The so-called bog-springs, of which there are 34 in number, rise in a small piece of boggy ground a little to the West of the sulphur-springs, and though close together no two are exactly alike'.

Fear that the town's image as a genteel resort was being tarnished was one of the reasons that the council members sought and were granted a Special Act of Parliament in 1893 to allow them to buy the Stray. Unregulated use of the Stray by itinerant concert parties, minstrel shows, quack doctors selling patent cure-alls, and firebrand evangelical ministers preaching to the masses, was all too much for the council. According to Alderman Fortune, council ownership would mean 'no circuses, no wild beast shows, no niggers holding their entertainments within 75 yards of any house'. Fear of loss of image was not confined to Harrogate. The residents of the spa's one-time greatest rival, Scarborough, objected to the coming of the railway on the grounds that it wanted nothing to do with the lower social orders: 'the watering place has no wish for a greater influx of vagrants and those who have no money to spend'.

At just under 21 miles from Whitby, Scarborough's career as a spa began after its waters were discovered by a certain Mrs Farrow in about 1626, though the earliest building over the well was little more than a wooden shelter built for the convenience of people drinking the waters. Disaster struck in 1737 when a landslip destroyed the spa; it was two years before it was able to be reopened. By this time, the spa was housed in a pump-room, but this too was destroyed and replaced in 1839. Harrogate's other Yorkshire rival was Ilkley, an obscure town until 1850 when the local spring waters were declared beneficial to health. Investment poured in as villas, hotels and hydros sprang up. Within a few years Ilkley was claiming to be the Malvern of the North. Taking the treatment at one of Ilkley's hydropathic establishments varied. The Ilkley Wells charged £3 3s a week; the Craig Lands £2 2s ; the Stone Lea £2 9s; the Troutbeck's rates were from 6s.6d a day; and the Rockwood and the Marlborough were 32s 6d a week. Prices were lower in the winter.

But the third most serious rival to

Harrogate was not in Yorkshire, but across the border in Derbyshire. With waters bubbling to the surface at a constant temperature of 82 degrees Fahrenheit, Buxton was something special in the north. By the 1570s Buxton was gaining a reputation as a spa, for the thermal waters were said to give relief from various aches and pains. In 1588, as the Spanish Armada was being forced by the prevailing winds into the North Sea, Queen Elizabeth charged her admirals to protect the realm, but not to spend too much money doing it, and promptly set off for Buxton to take the waters. It was thanks to the fifth Duke of Devonshire that Buxton was able to give even Bath a run for its money. Like Harrogate, Buxton is essentially divided into two: Higher Buxton, where the Market Place is to be found, and Lower Buxton, the area where the Crescent and Spring Gardens are. Lower Buxton in the 1840s was dominated by the imposing grandeur of the Crescent, built between 1780 and 1784, and the Great Stables, built in 1789. Both of these splendid buildings were designed by John Carr of York. But what the fifth Duke of Devonshire had started, the sixth and seventh Dukes continued. In the early-1850s the Baths were completely remodelled. The Hot Baths were rebuilt with an ornate glass and iron colonnade, and the Natural Baths were fitted out with public and private bathing facilities; the sexes were of course segregated. Buxton received a substantial boost to its fortunes on 30 May 1863 with the opening of two railway lines. The Midland Railway gave the town a direct route to and from London, while the Stockport, Disley & Whaley Bridge Railway allowed access to London & North Western routes. It was the railways that put the town on the tourist map, as well as cutting journey times for those coming to take the waters. Eager to capitalise on Buxton's popularity, the railway companies were soon offering weekend excursion tickets valid from Friday to the following Tuesday inclusive. Tourist tickets were offered from 1 May to 31 October, and remained valid until 31

December. Some of the return tourist fares charged for the 1887 season were: Aberdeen 101s 2d (1st class), 74s 1d (2nd class), 51s 10d (3rd class); Derby 9s 10d (1st class), 6s 1d (3rd class), London 43s 4d (1st class), 35s 4d (2nd class), 24s (3rd class); Bath 46s 10d (1st class) and 25s (3rd class). During the season through carriages were operated to London and back.

For Harrogate, the years immediately following the end of the Great War were boom years. Income from the baths and wells rocketed from £38,000 for 1918-19 to £59,000 in 1921-22. The general down-turn in the economy during 1922-23 saw income from treatments drop, but then it stabilised at £110,000 to £120,000 a year. Annual revenue from those coming to drink the waters continued at well above the £200,000 mark, with 259,000 tickets being issued during 1925-26. However, the council were concerned enough to send the manager of the Royal Baths on a fact-finding tour of continental spas. He reported that on the whole Harrogate was performing reasonably well. Only one major European spa, Vittel, was doing good business, but that was due to a massive investment programme. The council considered a number of options, including building a new Promenade Hall that would extend from the Royal Pump Room to the corner of the Victoria Baths.

The slump of 1929 hit the town hard. After operating for a number of years at a loss, the Victoria Baths was closed in 1930; it was such a sturdy building that it was converted for use as Municipal Offices. At the end of the 1930 season, another economy measure was the axing of the Municipal Orchestra, which was replaced with visits from the Hallé Orchestra. Income from the baths and wells fell. Revenue for 1929-30 was down to £41,200; during 1930-31 it dropped to £36,700. By 1932-33 both the Pump Room and the Royal Baths were operating at a loss, and the number of people coming for treatments was continuing to fall. However, unlike the situation in Buxton, the council did not roll over and play dead; they had the courage to invest in the town in an attempt to assist recovery. Money was invested in Valley Gardens. Projects included a new entrance and improved layout, and the building of the Sun Pavilion and Colonnade along the north side. Astute marketing and a sense of purpose in the 1930s helped the town develop into the premier conference centre in the country.

After the Second World War, modifications were carried out at the Royal Baths so that the NHS could use it for the treatment of rheumatism and other ailments. New facilities included a deep pool and a gymnasium. In 1952 the White Hart Hotel was bought by Leeds Regional Hospital Board and converted into a 130-bed hospital for walking patients. Its acquisition enabled the NHS to increase the number of treatments it could offer to between 100,000 and 120,000 a year. Though visitors for treatments continued to decline, Harrogate's geographical position - 204 miles from London and 175 miles from Edinburgh - made it an attractive location for conferences. By the mid 1950s the town was hosting 150 conferences a year; by the 1970s it was over 200, with the Royal Hall able to seat 1350 delegates, the Lounge Hall 750 and the Sun Pavilion 700. Harrogate is also a centre for festivals. The Spring Flower Show is considered to be one of the best in the country, and there are also drama and music festivals and an agricultural show.

OTEL
STATION HOTEL
Co. LTD
George Dalton

STATION SQUARE 1921 71649
The 45-bed Station Hotel, or North Eastern as it was usually called, was more for the passing trade than those coming to Harrogate for a week or two. The first railway to reach the town was the York & North Midland, with a branch from their main line at Church Fenton by way of Wetherby.

STATION SQUARE c1965 H26251
The focal point of Station Square is Queen Victoria's statue. It was erected in 1887 in honour of her jubilee.

JAMES STREET c1965 H26252
This is one of the principal shopping streets of the town. In 1911 Harrogate supported no fewer than 800 shops, and there was a time when major London retailers followed their wealthy clients to the spa, setting up for the season and then returning south. This was not unique to Harrogate; it certainly occurred at Clifton, near Bristol, at Bath, at Buxton, and at Scarborough.

James Street c1965 H26253
Cars line both sides of James Street. The previous year had seen record sales of private cars in the UK, with over 1,200,000 being sold. There was a down turn in 1965 with sales peaking at 1,148,000, possibly owing to higher taxes imposed by the Labour Government. The annual road fund licence also went up in 1965 from £15 to £17.10s.

George Dalton
TETLEY & SONS
CIGARS & TOBACCOS
GENTLEMEN'S HAIR DRESSING SALOONS
CIGARS TOBACCOS
SHAW'S

James Street 1914 67283
James Street forms one of the links between Station Parade and Parliament Square. Traffic is light enough for a road worker to get on with his job: no signs, no cones, no temporary traffic lights, no fuss, no health-and-safety risk assessment.

CAMBRIDGE STREET c1965 H26249

This photograph was taken from the junction with Market Street and looking towards St Peter's Church. High street chains include Woolworths, Burton, and Stylo. Back in the 1820s the town's businesses included Mrs Tiplady, who manufactured and sold ornamental whale bone; the studio of Mr George Wright, a miniature artist; and the fossil shop of Mr John Pearson.

THE KURSAAL 1911 63527

It was in 1898 that Dr Black first put forward proposals that Harrogate should build a Kursaal that would include a concert hall, newsroom and games rooms. Plans were drawn up in 1900 following a visit to the continent by a deputation; R J Beale and the great theatre architect Frank Matcham were commissioned to design the building.

The Kursaal 1907 58657

Frank Matcham (1854-1920) was one of the most prolific theatre architects of his day. Among his works were the Empire Palace, Hackney; Buxton Opera House; the Theatre Royal, Newcastle-upon-Tyne; and the New Hippodrome, Olympia. The Kursaal attracted world-class musicians; though it was subsidised for a number of years, on the eve of the Great War it was operating at a profit.

The Kursaal 1907 58656

Posters give notice that a sacred concert is to be held. These were a regular feature in spas and resorts around the country, as were open-air religious services. There is also a poster mentioning the daily concert given by the Municipal Orchestra. Formed in 1896 under J Sydney Jones, the orchestra survived until 1930, when it was disbanded as an economy measure.

The Royal Hall 1914 67287

In the Frith archive this picture is listed under the title of 'The Royal Hall', which indicates that it was either taken, or first published, after the outbreak of hostilities with Germany. At that time all things German were hurriedly renamed - and anti-German feelings even ran to the lower orders being encouraged to kick, or kill, dachshunds.

ROBERTS
8
R.A.ROBERTS

THE ROYAL HALL GARDENS 1925 78967
This is a popular place to sit and read or while away the time in conversation.

Parliament Street c1960 H26124

This view looks in the direction of the Royal Baths and Ripon Road. Among the businesses along here at the time were the Blue Bird Tea Rooms, Miss Bell the chiropodist, and Leonard Gill the stamp dealer. The Somerset Hotel, along with the Alexandra on Prospect Place and the Great Eastern, once enjoyed the reputation of being 'suitable for passing travellers'.

Parliament Street c1960 H26125

A policeman walks his beat in this busy street. Among the duties performed in the 1840s by Harrogate's first policeman was that of seeing that the mules and donkeys used for riding, or drawing small carriages about the town, were not abused by their owners or riders. In 1847 the two railway companies operating into Harrogate supplied two constables each to the town. The town policeman was promoted to the rank of Superintendent.

LOUIS COPE
Louis Cope

PARLIAMENT STREET 1923 74570
A policeman directs the traffic. The town's first policeman was appointed in 1841. He was paid a wage, but also received half the fines he collected - an early example of payment by results. From one unfortunate he earned 2s 9d: the poor man was fined 6d for emptying night-soil during the hours of daylight and a further 5s for using abusive language.

PARLIAMENT STREET 1907 58649

Harrogate's drug stores try and outdo one another with their advertising. On the right Taylor's Drug Store boldly displays its name in six-feet-high gilt lettering. Not to be outdone, the chemist directly across the street proclaims that his establishment is the largest in the world. Gilt lettering like this was popular with Victorian retailers, and when electric light became available many of these signs were modified so that they could be illuminated at night.

TAYLORS
DRUG
STORES
TYLER
SHOES
TAYLORS' DRUG STORES
CASH CHEMISTS
Y.M.C.A.
F. M. EVANS
TAYLORS

MAIN SQUARE c1965 H26233

Taylor's Drug Store is long gone. The ornate Victorian gilt lettering is but a memory, though it must have been impressive when compared to Timothy White's frontage. Happily, over on the left the ornate ironwork has managed to survive both developers and Second World War salvage drives.

PARLIAMENT STREET c1965 H26207

By the mid-1960s private car ownership was rising, and the ill-thought-out Beeching Plan would destroy much of the rail network. A hundred years or so before this picture was taken, it was the railways that not only brought in visitors, but made the town an attractive residential area for Leeds and Bradford businessmen.

PARLIAMENT SQUARE c1965 H26234

In the 1960s the high street banks had their branches around here. On Prospect Crescent were the Midland and Barclays; the Nat West and Lloyds could be found along Cambridge Crescent; whilst in James Street were the Yorkshire, York County, and a second branch of Barclays.

ST PETER'S CHURCH 1907 58658

Designed by J H Hirst, St Peter's was one of a number of places of worship to be built during the 1870s. The Methodists opened Cheltenham Mount (1873) and Trinity Wesleyan Chapel (1878). St Robert's Roman Catholic Church was built in 1873, and the Baptists opened a chapel in 1876. All Saints Chapel of Ease, Harlow Hill was opened in 1870.

ST PETER'S CHURCH 1927 80225
Hirst's original design of 1870-71 had included a tower, but this was not added until 1926. To the left of the church can be seen St Peter's School, which had originally been opened in 1865.

W. G. ALLEN & SON.

The War Memorial and Prospect Place 1923 74568
Harrogate's war memorial to those who gave their lives in the Great War is one of the more impressive monuments to that horrific conflict. The obelisk ranks along with the one erected at Southport as being among the largest of such monuments in the provinces.

PROSPECT PLACE 1911 63512

Most of the large hotels faced the Stray, including the Queen, the Granby, the Prince of Wales and the slightly smaller Empress. The Prospect Hotel, which is the building on the left, was described in one guidebook as being 'well situated, near the station, rooms from 4s 6d., dinner 6s'.

VIEW FROM THE PROSPECT HOTEL 1902 48970

Rates at the Prospect were similar to those at the Crown, the White Hart, and the Grand, which was opened in Cornwall Road in 1903. The most expensive at this time was probably the Majestic on Ripon Road. It was a huge establishment with grounds and a winter gardens; rates there started at 5s 6d for a room and 6s for dinner. The guidebooks of the day also warned tourists that it was the custom to dress for dinner at the more fashionable hotels.

PROSPECT HILL C1960 H26130

Prospect Hill is a handy thoroughfare for those wishing to travel between West Parade and Valley Gardens. The Prospect Hotel can be seen on the left towering above the trees.

THE STRAY 1888 20922

The 200-acre Stray was opened for public use in 1778, though a number of residents had rights, or gates as they were called, to pasture animals on it. A gate entitled its owner to right of pasture for one cow, or a two-year-old horse, or four sheep. There were fifty gates altogether, and these could be bought and sold or let for rent.

THE STRAY 1888 20923
Licensed carriages await their customers. In the 1840s a ban was imposed on carriages plying for hire on Sundays. However, a compromise was reached between the Hackney Carriage Committee and the cab drivers allowing them to ply on Sundays, but not during Divine Services.

FROM THE WHITE HART 1893 32012

Here to the right of the picture, we see the Prospect Hotel from the Stray. By the early 1890s unregulated use of the Stray was causing concern; minstrel shows, hustlers and quack doctors, itinerant preachers and so on were seen as a threat to Harrogate's image as a genteel resort. It was even noted that the ground in front of the Prospect Hotel had suffered so much from gatherings that it was quite bare of grass. The year this picture was taken a Special Act of Parliament was passed to allow the council to buy the Stray.

THE STRAY 1902 48967A

Many former stage and mail coaches went on to have second careers following their withdrawal from service; they were snapped up by operators for use on half or whole-day excursions. Favourite excursions from Harrogate around 1902 were to Knaresborough, Plumpton Park, Harewood, Ripon and Fountains Abbey.

The White Hart Hotel 1902 48971

Built to the south of Royal Parade in 1846, the White Hart, with its arched ground floor windows and Ionic columns either side of the front entrance, was the first large hotel in the town. It is considered by many to be one of Harrogate's finest buildings. In the early 1950s it was acquired by the NHS and converted into a 130-bed hospital for walking patients.

Christ Church 1938 88346

Situated between Skipton Road and Park Parade, Christ Church was designed by John Oates and built in 1831. By the late 1850s it was too small to meet the needs of both the local congregation and visitors wishing to worship. Lockwood & Mawson of Bradford were commissioned to design the transepts; these were built in 1862, giving Christ Church an additional 240 seats.

ST WILFRED'S CHURCH 1928 81541
Designed by Temple Moore in an Early English style, St Wilfred's was built between 1905 and 1914. Leslie Moore, the architect's nephew, added the tower-like north transept and apsidal south transept in 1928, the Church Hall in 1934, and the Lady Chapel in 1935.

VICTORIA SQUARE 1935 87160
Built on the corner of Albert Street and Station Parade, the United Methodist Free Church was another of Bristol architect J H Hirst's Harrogate buildings. The church could hold 700 worshippers, and there was a schoolroom for 200. The site was later redeveloped for retail use.

St Mary's Church 1891 28311
Built in 1824-25, St Mary's was originally a chapel within the parish of Pannal. Capable of seating 500 worshippers, and heavily refurbished during the 1890s, St Mary's was considered too small by 1900. A new site was acquired off Cold Bath Road where a temporary iron church was erected in 1903. The new church opened in 1916.

The Adelphi Hotel 1924 75646
The AA-appointed 90-bed Adelphi Hotel was in a similar price band to the Wellington and the George. Other AA-appointed hotels were the Majestic, the Prince of Wales, the Clarendon and the Grand. The George was RAC-listed, along with the Lancaster and the Clarendon. The Auto Cycle Union favoured the Three Horse Shoes.

HARLOW MANOR HYDRO 1902 48986

Built in 1875 by Leeds-based architect John Milling as his private residence, Harlow Manor was converted into a hydropathic establishment in 1893. Hydropathic treatments were developed during the 1830s by Vincenz Priessnitz, who combined the use of cold water with dietary regimes and abstinence from alcohol. Hydros offered a wide range of treatments using ordinary water; these included the lumbar douche, the spleenic douche, douche massage, electric baths, the Greville hot-air treatment, Nauheim treatment for affections of the heart, Turkish baths, sitz baths and the surge bath.

THE CAIRN HYDRO 1928 81537

During the last quarter of the 19th century a number of hydros opened; the first was the Harrogate Hydropathic (formerly the Swan Hotel) in 1878. There were three large establishments, the Harrogate, the Cairn (1892), and the Harlow Manor (1893), and several smaller ones, including the Connaught and the Imperial.

THE VICTORIA BATHS 1888 20940

After operating at a loss for several years, the slump of 1929 was the final straw for the Victoria Baths. It closed in 1930, but it was such a solid building that it was refurbished, given a new facade, and re-opened in 1931 as the Municipal Offices.

THE ROYAL PUMP ROOM 1907 58650

The Royal Pump Room opened at 7.00am, dispensing bumpers of sulphuric and chalybeate water. The roads leading to the Pump Room were chained off so as to allow drinkers the opportunity of enjoying a leisurely constitutional in either the Crescent or Valley Gardens.

The Royal Pump Room 1914 67285
The busiest day ever recorded at the Royal Pump Room was during the 1926 season, when 1500 people were served in one morning. This picture shows the Pump Room extension added in 1913.

CRESCENT GARDENS 1911 63514

Two elegantly dressed ladies enjoy a stroll in the sunshine as the crowd gathers around the bandstand. During the season visitors would take the waters at the Pump Room, then make their way here for a concert. Late morning concerts were also held in the Winter Gardens.

THE ROYAL BATHS 1935 87157
Here we see the Royal Baths from Crescent Gardens. When they first opened in 1897, these baths were said to be unequalled in decoration and roominess, and for 5s 6d it was possible to enjoy a 'mud bath' with electricity.

THE NEW BATHS 1897 39430
The Royal Baths cost nearly £100,000 to build in 1897; even the Kursaal, which opened in 1903, cost over £70,000. The money lavished on providing Harrogate with the best spa facilities in the country was well spent; it ensured that the town remained the most fashionable of all the spas for fifty years.

Entrance to Valley Gardens c1965 H26202

The Annual Flower Show was established in 1843, and for many years it was held in the grounds of the Cheltenham Spa. Flower shows were once an important element, for they reinforced a resort's status. Another famous flower show is Southport's, which was first staged by its corporation in 1924 to promote the resort's garden city image.

Entrance to Valley Gardens 1914 67286

The young boy in his shirt-sleeves and the lady using her umbrella indicates that the picture might have been taken during the high hot summer. On Sunday 28 June, as Lancashire and Yorkshire enjoyed their hottest day of the year, the heir to the throne of the Austro-Hungarian Empire, Franz Ferdinand, and his wife were assassinated in Sarajevo, Bosnia. Soon Europe would be aflame and millions would make the ultimate sacrifice.

THE PUMP ROOM FROM VALLEY GARDENS 1928 81527
Along with the Crescent Gardens, which are situated between the Pump Room and the Municipal Offices (Victoria Baths), the Valley Gardens offers visitors a garden walk of nearly one mile in length from Low Harrogate to the heights of Harlow Moor.

The Pump Room from Valley Gardens 1928 81526
The Frith cameraman heads deeper, though not that much deeper, into Valley Gardens. From our records it appears that our man was sent to Harrogate in 1928 specifically to photograph the Gardens, yet for some reason, now forgotten, no one was sent in 1933 to photograph the newly-completed Sun Pavilion and Colonnade.

VALLEY GARDENS ENTRANCE 1928 81523

VALLEY GARDENS ENTRANCE 1928
In the 1920s approximate mean temperature, rainfall and sunshine figures for the West Riding listed Harrogate has having 197 days of rain, 1442 days of sunshine and a temperature range between January and July of 36.6F. The driest month was April.

VALLEY DRIVE AND GARDENS 1928
Extending from the Pump Room to Harlow Moor, Valley Gardens at this time features well-thought-out flower beds and borders, lawns, trees, and tennis courts. In 1933, in an effort to promote recovery of the spa, the Sun Pavilion and Colonnade were built along the north side of the gardens.

VALLEY DRIVE AND GARDENS 1928 81508

VALLEY GARDENS 1907 58645A
The white silk shirts and dunce's caps leave us in no doubt that this is a Pierrot troupe. This type of entertainment owed its popularity to the runaway success of the London production of the mime play 'L'Enfant Prodigue' in 1891 in which the character of Pierrot featured. The act would feature songs, jokes, mime and monologues.

VALLEY GARDENS, THE TEA HOUSE 1911 63516

The Tea House was one of the focal points of the Valley Gardens; friends and family would often arrange to meet here, and they could enjoy refreshments served in the 'continental manner'. In many towns, visitors to public parks were forbidden to bring their own food and drink, and picnics were not allowed under any circumstances whatsoever.

VALLEY GARDENS 1924 75639

We have no real idea what is going on here, but the fact that people are standing and the gentlemen have removed their hats indicates that the national anthem is being played.

THE BANDSTAND, VALLEY GARDENS 1925 78972
For decades music has featured in the life of Harrogate. The area around the bandstand is packed for an afternoon concert, just one of a number given daily about the town. Other locations were the Winter Gardens, the Royal Hall, and the Royal Baths Assembly Rooms.

Valley Gardens, the Bandstand and Tea House 1928 81513
Though the Gardens look crowded, coming to Harrogate to take the waters was already in decline by 1928. Drugs and dietary regimes were replacing spa treatments for many ailments such as gout and anaemia.

The Children's Pool 1925 78971
Adults keep a watchful eye on the budding yachting enthusiasts among the younger members of their respective families. In those pre-radio control days, sail boats were all that there was on offer.

VALLEY GARDENS 1928 81516
There are 88 wells around Harrogate, many of them within Valley Gardens, where they are covered with circular stones. Though wells might be only a few metres apart, their waters are never the same.

The Royal Bath Hospital 1892 30627

The Royal Bath Hospital 1892
The 150-bed Royal Bath Hospital and Rawson Convalescent Home, Cornwall Road, was built in 1888-89 at a cost of around £50,000. It was built on the site of the original 40-bed hospital of 1826; the convalescent wing was paid for by Miss Elizabeth Rawson and the Hon H E Butler of Nidd Hall.

Birk Crag
Elephant Rock 1921
Exercise was an integral part of taking the cure. Harrogate, like Ilkley and Buxton, was noted for the surrounding countryside and its cool and salubrious air.

Birk Crag, Elephant Rock 1921 71660

Knaresborough, The Town and the River 1888 20944

The church on the right is St John's, which dates from the 13th and 14th centuries. For centuries the tower bore traces of burning, testament to an attempt by Scots raiders in 1318 to destroy it. The Scots breached the town's ditch and palisade defences and burned between 140 and 160 properties. The church contains a monument to Sir William Slingsby, who discovered the first springs at Harrogate.

Knaresborough, The Town and the River 1888 20946

The royal borough of Knaresborough is perched on the summit of a hill overlooking the River Nidd. No one is sure how long the area has been inhabited; there have been finds of Roman coins, and some believe that Knaresborough might have originated as an Anglo-Saxon fortified settlement. The distinctive railway viaduct is the second to span the Nidd. The first collapsed shortly after completion in 1847, but was soon replaced.

Knaresborough, The River Nidd 1914 67266
Boating on this stretch of the Nidd has been a popular leisure activity for decades. It was no different in 1914.

Knaresborough, The Castle 1892 30611
The first castle on the site is thought to have been begun by Serlo de Burg, who received lands in the area for services rendered to William the Conqueror. The fortress was extensively rebuilt during the early decades of the 14th century, and was probably started around 1310 after the lordship had been granted by Edward II to his favourite, and possible lover, Piers Gaveston.

KNARESBOROUGH, THE FERRY TO THE DROPPING WELL 1911 63532
The floating tea rooms appears to be doing a brisk trade, as does the ferry to the Dropping Well. On the hill above the town stands the ruins of Knaresborough Castle. In April 1646 Parliament issued its first instruction that the fortress be made untenable, though it was not stripped of its garrison until some time after February 1647. Substantial demolition was undertaken under the directions of the County Committee from October 1648.

KNARESBOROUGH, 'MOTHER SHIPTON INN' 1914 67264
This was a popular place with motorists from far and wide, though when this picture was taken the Dropping Well was being patronised by locals - AK1575 is a Bradford registration and C74 is a Yorkshire West Riding plate. The well is a petrifying well, similar to those at Matlock Bath in Derbyshire. Over a period of several weeks the limestone deposits in the spring water solidify any objects placed into it. The star attraction here used to be a petrified mongoose.

KNARESBOROUGH, THE OLD CHEMIST'S SHOP 1911 63543

Though Knaresborough boasts the oldest chemist's shop in England, it does not hold the record for keeping its shutters up. That unique record is held by Ye Olde Chymist Shoppe of Forster & Co, Clayton Street, Newcastle-upon-Tyne. Known locally as Dirty Dicks, Forster's opened in 1840. It closed for good in 1972, having never taken its shutters down in over 100 years.

KNARESBOROUGH, THE OLD CHEMIST'S SHOP 1914 67279

Note the pestles and mortars used by Mr Lawrence, the apothecary in charge for grinding ingredients for remedies. Until 1840 some of this work was done in a large dog-powered pestle and mortar.

KNARESBOROUGH, MARKET DAY 1921 71687
Plenty of local produce is on sale here, with apples at 9d a half stone and beans 5d a pound; potatoes are a bargain at 5d a half stone, as in high street shops they were around 2d a pound. Cucumbers are on offer at 6d each; stewing pears at 4d a pound; and tomatoes at 9d a pound.

MASON
GROCERIES A. BEAL

KNARESBOROUGH, HIGH STREET 1921 71682

In the days of mail and stagecoaches, the High Street was often the scene of frantic activity. The coach for Selby left from the Bay Horse, while those for Thirsk, Leeds, York and Harrogate used the Elephant & Castle. A waggon service to York was operated from the Black Swan, running on Mondays, Wednesdays and Fridays.

HAMPSTHWAITE, THE VILLAGE c1960 H190010

In the Honour of Knaresborough, Hampsthwaite was held by the Crown. In 1304 Edward I granted the village a four-day fair to be held annually during the feast of St Thomas the Martyr; Pannal was granted similar rights for the feast of St Michael.

HAMPSTHWAITE, HIGH STREET c1960 H190037

In the 1820s the village had three pubs: the Joiners Arms, the Lamb, and the Nelson Inn. In earlier times a frequent visitor to Mary Thackwray's alehouse was Samuel Sugden, vicar of Hampsthwaite from 1670 to 1686. In 1682 Sugden was accused of tavern haunting, brawling and immorality. After one heavy session Sugden was crawling on all fours back to the vicarage when he was met by Catherine Hardcastle, wife of a Harrogate butcher. Though in no fit state, Sugden immediately propositioned Mrs Hardcastle and invited her to join him under a hedge.

HAMPSTHWAITE, THE VILLAGE c1960 H190038

Hampsthwaite was Nidderdale's pioneer when it came to long-term planning to assist its poor, old and infirm. Until 1622, moneys left for the poor in Nidderdale had with but one exception been for immediate disbursement. Anthony Craven of Darley changed that. He proposed that a fund for poor relief be established, and that only accrued interest be given out. He started the ball rolling with £5, and over the years this was added to, thanks to bequests from other people. The idea caught on, and similar schemes were started at Ripley, Fewston and Birstwith.

HAMPSTHWAITE, THE VILLAGE c1955 H190020

Here we see a very quiet Hampsthwaite on a summer morning in the mid-1950s. On the left is the shop belonging to a boot and shoe repairer and clog maker. In 1820 there were four shoemakers in the village: William Bramley, William Hodgson, John Rinder and John Sidgworth. The village also boasted two wheelwrights, a blacksmith, a schoolmaster, and a surgeon.

Hampsthwaite, The Village c1960 H190005
Milk churns by the lorry load are passing through. Between 1880 and 1900 the number of non-dairy cattle on Nidderdale farms fell, but there was an increase in milk cows. The reason given is the increased demand for milk caused by the rise in population in the Harrogate area. During this period, the housing stock in Harrogate rose from 950 dwellings to over 2800.

Hampsthwaite, High Street c1960 H190036
The Forest of Knaresborough, in which Hampsthwaite lay, was scheduled for enclosure by the Duchy of Lancaster in the mid-1760s. The Forest was surveyed during 1766-67 to access how many cottages had been built and how many encroachments had taken place without a licence from the Duchy. An anti-enclosure meeting was held in the village, where a petition attracted 169 signatures. It was later discovered that most of the petitioners were illegal encroachers or cottagers.

HAMPSTHWAITE, THE CHURCH c1955 H190030

HAMPSTHWAITE
The Church c1955

The church of St Thomas Becket was once a dependency of the mother church at Aldborough. Eventually, this large parish was broken up and Hampsthwaite became a parish in its own right; its territory extended west as far as Padside. The church was reconstructed in the 1820s and rebuilt in 1902.

BIRSTWITH
The Village c1960

Situated three miles south-west of Ripley, Birstwith had a population of over 600 in the early 1820s. Leading villagers at the time were farmer Robert Robinson; corn miller and cotton manufacturer John Greenwood; linen manufacturer Edward Spence; grocer and draper Joseph Spence; and schoolmaster Robert Stothart.

BIRSTWITH, THE VILLAGE c1960 B338008

Birstwith, The Village c1960 B338006

In the 17th century there were a number of Quakers living in Nidderdale, many of them in the areas around Hartwith, Winsley, Birstwith, Fellbeck, Hampsthwaite, Pateley Bridge, Dacre and Brimham. They were heavily persecuted following the Restoration, and Acts passed in 1662 and 1664 forbade gatherings of more than five persons for any form of worship not authorised by law. John Spence of Menwith and Michael Brunskill of Hampsthwaite were among the Quakers who died in York Castle following their imprisonment for refusing to pay tithes.

Birstwith, The Post Office and Stores c1960 B338012

The first recorded financial support given to the villagers is in 1635, when Thomas Skaife left £10 invested in stock for poor relief, and a penny dole for everyone who attended his funeral. By the late 18th century Birstwith was making regular payments to those who needed them. The old and infirm received between 3s 6d and 5s a month; a widow with children 4s; and a sick couple 12s. Many got their rent paid and midwives' fees and funeral expenses met.

BIRSTWITH, THE CHURCH c1960 B338011

BIRSTWITH
The Church c1960

By 1851 Nidderdale was predominantly Methodist; both the Wesleyans and Primitives had a number of chapels. Birstwith's Anglicans did not have their own church until 1856-57, when one was built despite opposition from Thomas Shann, vicar of Hampsthwaite.

BIRSTWITH
The Waterfall c1960

Water once played an important role in the economy of the Forest. In 1086, with much of the land laid waste, the Domesday Commissioners reported that the only mills operating in the area were at Spofforth and Great Braham. By the 14th century things were much improved; there were mills at Hampsthwaite, Killinghall and Bilton Mills on the Nidd, and others at Washburn, Darley Beck and Crimple Beck.

BIRSTWITH, THE WATERFALL c1960 B338003

Index

Frith Book Co Titles

Frith Book Company publish over a 100 new titles each year. For latest catalogue please contact Frith Book Co.

Town Books 96pp, 100 photos. County and Themed Books 128pp, 150 photos (unless specified) All titles hardback laminated case and jacket except those indicated pb (paperback)

Title	ISBN	Price
Around Barnstaple	1-85937-084-5	£12.99
Around Blackpool	1-85937-049-7	£12.99
Around Bognor Regis	1-85937-055-1	£12.99
Around Bristol	1-85937-050-0	£12.99
Around Cambridge	1-85937-092-6	£12.99
Cheshire	1-85937-045-4	£14.99
Around Chester	1-85937-090-X	£12.99
Around Chesterfield	1-85937-071-3	£12.99
Around Chichester	1-85937-089-6	£12.99
Cornwall	1-85937-054-3	£14.99
Cotswolds	1-85937-099-3	£14.99
Around Derby	1-85937-046-2	£12.99
Devon	1-85937-052-7	£14.99
Dorset	1-85937-075-6	£14.99
Dorset Coast	1-85937-062-4	£14.99
Around Dublin	1-85937-058-6	£12.99
East Anglia	1-85937-059-4	£14.99
Around Eastbourne	1-85937-061-6	£12.99
English Castles	1-85937-078-0	£14.99
Around Falmouth	1-85937-066-7	£12.99
Hampshire	1-85937-064-0	£14.99
Isle of Man	1-85937-065-9	£14.99
Around Maidstone	1-85937-056-X	£12.99
North Yorkshire	1-85937-048-9	£14.99
Around Nottingham	1-85937-060-8	£12.99
Around Penzance	1-85937-069-1	£12.99
Around Reading	1-85937-087-X	£12.99
Around St Ives	1-85937-068-3	£12.99
Around Salisbury	1-85937-091-8	£12.99
Around Scarborough	1-85937-104-3	£12.99
Scottish Castles	1-85937-077-2	£14.99
Around Sevenoaks and Tonbridge	1-85937-057-8	£12.99
Sheffield and S Yorkshire	1-85937-070-5	£14.99
Shropshire	1-85937-083-7	£14.99
Staffordshire	1-85937-047-0 (96pp)	£12.99
Suffolk	1-85937-074-8	£14.99
Surrey	1-85937-081-0	£14.99
Torbay	1-85937-063-2	£12.99
Wiltshire	1-85937-053-5	£14.99
Around Bakewell	1-85937-1132	£12.99
Around Bournemouth	1-85937-067-5	£12.99
Cambridgeshire	1-85937-086-1	£14.99
Essex	1-85937-082-9	£14.99
Around Great Yarmouth	1-85937-085-3	£12.99
Hertfordshire	1-85937-079-9	£14.99
Isle of Wight	1-85937-114-0	£14.99
Around Lincoln	1-85937-111-6	£12.99
Oxfordshire	1-85937-076-4	£14.99
Around Shrewsbury	1-85937-110-8	£12.99
South Devon Coast	1-85937-107-8	£14.99
Around Stratford upon Avon	1-85937-098-5	£12.99
West Midlands	1-85937-109-4	£14.99

British Life A Century Ago
246 x 189mm
144pp, hardback.
Black and white
Lavishly illustrated with photos from the turn of the century, and with extensive commentary. It offers a unique insight into the social history and heritage of bygone Britain.
1-85937-103-5 £17.99

Available from your local bookshop or from the publisher

Frith Book Co Titles Available in 2000

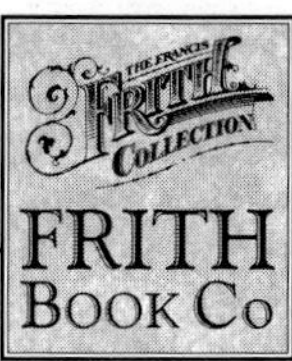

Title	ISBN	Price	Month
Around Bath	1-85937-097-7	£12.99	Mar
County Durham	1-85937-123-x	£14.99	Mar
Cumbria	1-85937-101-9	£14.99	Mar
Down the Thames	1-85937-121-3	£14.99	Mar
Around Exeter	1-85937-126-4	£12.99	Mar
Greater Manchester	1-85937-108-6	£14.99	Mar
Around Guildford	1-85937-117-5	£12.99	Mar
Around Harrogate	1-85937-112-4	£12.99	Mar
Around Leicester	1-85937-073-x	£12.99	Mar
Around Liverpool	1-85937-051-9	£12.99	Mar
Around Newark	1-85937-105-1	£12.99	Mar
Northumberland and Tyne & Wear	1-85937-072-1	£14.99	Mar
Around Oxford	1-85937-096-9	£12.99	Mar
Around Plymouth	1-85937-119-1	£12.99	Mar
Around Southport	1-85937-106-x	£12.99	Mar
Welsh Castles	1-85937-120-5	£14.99	Mar
Around Belfast	1-85937-094-2	£12.99	Apr
Canals and Waterways	1-85937-129-9	£17.99	Apr
Down the Severn	1-85937-118-3	£14.99	Apr
East Sussex	1-85937-130-2	£14.99	Apr
Exmoor	1-85937-132-9	£14.99	Apr
Gloucestershire	1-85937-102-7	£14.99	Apr
Around Horsham	1-85937-127-2	£12.99	Apr
Around Ipswich	1-85937-133-7	£12.99	Apr
Ireland (pb)	1-85937-181-7	£9.99	Apr
Kent Living Memories	1-85937-125-6	£14.99	Apr
London (pb)	1-85937-183-3	£9.99	Apr
New Forest	1-85937-128-0	£14.99	Apr
Scotland (pb)	1-85937-182-5	£9.99	Apr
Around Southampton	1-85937-088-8	£12.99	Apr
Stone Circles & Ancient Monuments	1-85937-143-4	£17.99	Apr
Sussex (pb)	1-85937-184-1	£9.99	Apr
Colchester (pb)	1-85937-188-4	£8.99	May
County Maps of Britain	1-85937-156-6 (192pp)	£19.99	May
Leicestershire (pb)	1-85937-185-x	£9.99	May
Lincolnshire	1-85937-135-3	£14.99	May
Around Newquay	1-85937-140-x	£12.99	May
Nottinghamshire (pb)	1-85937-187-6	£9.99	May
Redhill to Reigate	1-85937-137-x	£12.99	May
Victorian & Edwardian Yorkshire	1-85937-154-x	£14.99	May
Around Winchester	1-85937-139-6	£12.99	May
Yorkshire (pb)	1-85937-186-8	£9.99	May
Berkshire (pb)	1-85937-191-4	£9.99	Jun
Brighton (pb)	1-85937-192-2	£8.99	Jun
Dartmoor	1-85937-145-0	£14.99	Jun
East London	1-85937-080-2	£14.99	Jun
Glasgow (pb)	1-85937-190-6	£8.99	Jun
Kent (pb)	1-85937-189-2	£9.99	Jun
Victorian & Edwardian Kent	1-85937-149-3	£14.99	Jun
North Devon Coast	1-85937-146-9	£14.99	Jun
Peak District	1-85937-100-0	£14.99	Jun
Around Truro	1-85937-147-7	£12.99	Jun
Victorian & Edwardian Maritime Album	1-85937-144-2	£14.99	Jun
West Sussex	1-85937-148-5	£14.99	Jun
Churches of Berkshire	1-85937-170-1	£17.99	Jul
Churches of Dorset	1-85937-172-8	£17.99	Jul
Churches of Hampshire	1-85937-207-4	£17.99	Jul
Churches of Wiltshire	1-85937-171-x	£17.99	Jul
Derbyshire (pb)	1-85937-196-5	£9.99	Jul
Edinburgh	1-85937-193-0	£8.99	Jul
Herefordshire	1-85937-174-4	£14.99	Jul
Norwich (pb)	1-85937-194-9	£8.99	Jul
Ports and Harbours	1-85937-208-2	£17.99	Jul
Somerset and Avon	1-85937-153-1	£14.99	Jul
South Devon Living Memories	1-85937-168-x	£14.99	Jul
Warickshire`	1-85937-203-1	£9.99	Jul
Worcestershire	1-85937-152-3	£14.99	Jul
Yorkshire Living Memories	1-85937-166-3	£14.99	Jul

Frith Products & Services

Francis Frith would doubtless be pleased to know that the pioneering publishing venture he started in 1860 still continues today. More than a hundred and thirty years later, The Francis Frith Collection continues in the same innovative tradition and is now one of the foremost publishers of vintage photographs in the world. Some of the current activities include:

Interior Decoration

Today Frith's photographs can be seen framed and as giant wall murals in thousands of pubs, restaurants, hotels, banks, retail stores and other public buildings throughout the country. In every case they enhance the unique local atmosphere of the places they depict and provide reminders of gentler days in an increasingly busy and frenetic world.

Product Promotions

Frith products have been used by many major companies to promote the sales of their own products or to reinforce their own history and heritage. Brands include Hovis bread, Courage beers, Scots Porage Oats, Colman's mustard, Cadbury's foods, Mellow Birds coffee, Dunhill pipe tobacco, Guinness, and Bulmer's Cider.

Genealogy and Family History

As the interest in family history and roots grows world-wide, more and more people are turning to Frith's photographs of Great Britain for images of the towns, villages and streets where their ancestors lived; and, of course, photographs of the churches and chapels where their ancestors were christened, married and buried are an essential part of every genealogy tree and family album.

A series of easy-to-use CD Roms is planned for publication, and an increasing number of Frith photographs will be able to be viewed on specialist genealogy sites. A growing range of Frith books will be available on CD.

The Internet

Already thousands of Frith photographs can be viewed and purchased on the internet. By the end of the year 2000 some 60,000 Frith photographs will be available on the internet. The number of sites is constantly expanding, each focussing on different products and services from the Collection.

Some of the sites are listed below.

www.townpages.co.uk
www.icollector.com
www.barclaysquare.co.uk
www.cornwall-online.co.uk

For background information on the Collection look at the three following sites:

www.francisfrith.com
www.francisfrith.co.uk
www.frithbook.co.uk

Frith Products

All Frith photographs are available Framed or just as Mounted Prints, and can be ordered from the address below. From time to time other products - Address Books, Calendars, Table Mats, Postcards etc - are available.

The Frith Collectors' Guild

In response to the many customers who enjoy collecting Frith photographs we have created the Frith Collectors' Guild. Members are entitled to a range of benefits, including a regular magazine, special discounts and special limited edition products.

For further information: if you would like further information on any of the above aspects of the Frith business please contact us at the address below:

The Francis Frith Collection, Frith's Barn, Teffont, Salisbury, Wiltshire England SP3 5QP.
Tel: +44 (0) 1722 716 376 Fax: +44 (0) 1722 716 881 Email: uksales@francisfrith.com